MASTERS OF MUSIC
JAZZ
AND ITS HISTORY

TEXT BY
GIUSEPPE VIGNA

ILLUSTRATIONS BY
STUDIO BONI-PIERI-CRITONE

BARRON'S

DoGi

English translation ©
Copyright 1999
by Barron's Educational
Series, Inc.
Original edition © 1998 by
DoGi spa Florence Italy
Title of original edition:
Il jazz e la sua storia
Italian edition by:
Guiseppe Vigna
Revision by:
Leonardo Bonechi
Graphic Display:
Francesco Lo Bello
Illustrations:
Studio Boni-Pieri-Critone
Art director:
Sebastiano Ranchetti
Page make-up:
Katherine Carson Forden
Sebastiano Ranchetti
Iconographic researcher:
Katherine Carson Forden
Editorial Staff:
Andrea Bachini
Translation from Italian by:
Anna Maria Salmeri Pherson

HOW TO READ THIS BOOK

*Every facing page is a chapter on the environments,
the protagonists, the instruments
or the great moments of the history of jazz.
The text above on the left (1) and the large*
*illustration in the middle present the main
subject. The other elements of the page—
photos, reproductions of prints of epoch, and
portraits—complement the information.*

ACKNOWLEDGMENTS

ABBREVIATIONS: t: top / b: bottom / c: center / r: right / l: left

ILLUSTRATIONS: The illustrations in this volume are new and original. They have been realized upon project and supervision of DoGi spa, which owns its copyright.
DESIGNING by Studio Boni-Pieri-Critone, Lucia Mattioli, Armando Ponzecchi, and Alessandro Rabatti
Cover by Luciano Crovato and Gianni Mazzoleni (center) and Luigi Critone
BACK COVER by Luigi Critone

LIST OF REPRODUCTIONS:
DoGi spa has done its best to discover possible rights of third parties. We apologize for any omissions or mistakes that might have occurred, and we will be pleased to introduce the appropriate corrections in the later editions of this book. We would like to thank the Library of North American History and Literature at the History Department of the University of Florence.

(The works reproduced in their integrity are followed by the consonant t; those partially reproduced are followed by the consonant p.)
6l Anonymous, *View of French Cape and the Boat Le Marie Seraphique of Nantes,* end of 1700, watercolor (NANTES, MUSEE DES SALORGES) p; **6tr** Anonymous, *The Slave Trade,* engraving (IGDA-RIZZOLI, MILAN) t; **7tl** E. Jahn, *The First Battle of Bull Run in the Civil War,* print from Eslon's Civil War (PHOTO MARY EVANS PICTURE LIBRARY, LONDON) t; **8tl** *A Cotton Flower,* colored engraving (PHOTO MARY EVANS PICTURE LIBRARY, LONDON) t; **11tr** *A Troupe of Minstrels,* early 1900s (ARCHIVE DoGi, FLORENCE) p; **12t** *Robert Johnson* (DIME STORE PHOTO) p; **13tl** *Bessie Smith* (ARCHIVE NORDISK) p; **13tr** *Sheet Music of Maple Leaf Rag* by Scott Joplin (ARCHIVE ALVAR) t; **14bl** *A Riverboat,* colored lithograph (ARCHIVE CURRIER & IVES) t; **14tr** *King Oliver* (IGDA, MILAN) t; **15tr** *A Street in Storyville* (ARCHIVE MAX JONES) p; **16tl** *Louis Armstrong* (RCS-IGDA, MILAN) t; **17tr** *Bix Beiderbecke* (ARCHIVE MAX JONES) t; **18tl** *Jelly Roll Morton* (ARCHIVE ALVAR) p; **18bl** Cover of the edition *Hot Jazz* by Jelly Roll Morton (PHOTO FEDERICO GONZALES) p; **19tr** *Fletcher Henderson* (FBA, MILAN) p; **20t** *Alcoholic beverages confiscated at Luigi's,* January 1923 (PHOTO MUSEUM OF THE CITY OF NEW YORK, NEW YORK) t; **21tr** *George Gershwin* (PHOTO MICHAEL OCHS ARCHIVES/REDFERNS, LONDON) p; **21br** *F. Scott Fitzgerald,* circa 1925 (SNAP PHOTO/JR/GRAZIA NERI, MILAN) p; **22t** *Cotton Club* (PHOTO JAZZ MUSIC; RUSCONI PUBLISHER) t; **23tl** *Cab Calloway* (PHOTO ROLF DAHLGREN) t; **23tc** *Fats Waller* (FRANK DRIGGS COLLECTION) p; **23tr** *Duke Ellington* (FRANK DRIGGS COLLECTION) p; **24l** *Django Reinhardt* (FRANK DRIGGS COLLECTION) p; **25tr** *Sidney Bechet* (PHOTO BERYLE BEMOEN) p; **26t** *Count Basie* (ARCHIVE BARAZZETTA) t; **27tl** *Lester Young* (PHOTO FBS, MILAN) p; **27tc** *Roy Eldridge* (FRANK DRIGGS COLLECTION) p; **27tr** Cover by Billie Holiday at *Jazz at the Philharmonic* (CLEF RECORDS) p; **27br** *Art Tatum* (FRANK DRIGGS COLLECTION) p; **29tr** *Benny Goodman* (IGDA, MILAN) p; **29b** *Carnegie Hall,* engraving, Alfred Scott Publisher (CARNEGIE HALL ARCHIVES, NEW YORK) t; **30l** *Baby Dodds* (PHOTO JAZZ MUSIC; RUSCONI PUBLISHER) p; **31tr** *Kenny Clarke* (PHOTO HERMAN LEONARD) p; **31br** *Elvin Jones* (PHOTO BRIAN FOSKETT) p; **31bl** *Jo Jones* (PHOTO VERYL C. OAKLAND) p; **32t** *Coleman Hawkins* (FBS, MILAN) p; **33tr** *Cassandra Wilson* (PHOTO EBET ROBERTS/REDFERNS, LONDON) t; **34tl** *Billie Holiday* (PHOTO WILLIAM GOTTLIEB/REDFERNS, LONDON) p; **34tr** *Carmen McRae* (PHOTO JAZZ MUSIC, RUSCONI PUBLISHER) p; **35tc** *Frank Sinatra* (RCS-IGDA, MILAN) p; **35tr** *Louis Armstrong* (ARCHIVE RBA-POGGI, MILAN) p; **36t** *Glenn Miller* (PHOTO GIAN CARLO RONCAGLIERE) p; **37tl** *The Allies' Victory,* 1943, Naples (PHOTO ROBERT CAPA/AGENZIA CONTRASTO, ROME) t; **37tr** Original V-Disc Collection Cover (RUSCONI PUBLISHER) t; **38tl** *Charlie Parker* (ARCHIVE RBA, MILAN) p; **38tr** *Charlie Christian* (FRANK DRIGGS COLLECTION) p; **39tr** *Dizzy Gillespie* (FBS, MILAN) p; **39b** *Bud Powell* (PHOTO VAL WILMER) p; **40tl** *Elvis Presley* (ARCHIVE CURCIO, ROME) p; **40b** *Keith Richards* (ARCHIVE CURCIO, ROME) p; **41tl** *Ray Charles* (PHOTO DAVID REDFERN/REDFERNS, LONDON) t; **41tc** *James Brown* (PHOTO DAVID REDFERN/REDFERNS, LONDON) t; **42t** *The Quartet of Gerry Mulligan and Chet Baker* (ARCHIVE RBA, MILAN) p; **42bl** *The Modern Jazz Quartet* (PHOTO HERMAN LEONARD) p; **43tr** *Lennie Tristano* (PHOTO BOB PARENT) t; **44tl** *Collection of Records* (PRIVATE COLLECTION, FLORENCE) t; **47tr** Cover of the Edition *Ellington at Newport* (CBS JAZZ MASTERPIECES) t; **48tl** *Sonny Rollins* (MOSAIC IMAGES) p; **48c** *Art Blakey* (FBS, MILAN) p; **48b** *Bill Evans* (PHOTO DAVID REDFERN/REDFERENS, LONDON) p; **49tr** *Thelonious Monk* (PHOTO BRIAN FOSKETT) p; **50tl** *Charles Mingus* (PHOTO GIANCARLO RONCAGLIA) p; **51** Cover of the edition *We Insist! Max Roach's Freedom Now Suite* (AMIGO MUSIKPRODUKTION; PHOTO HUGH BELL) t; **52tl** *Ornette Coleman* (PHOTO ELIGIO PAONI/AGENZIA CONTRASTO, ROME) t; **52c** *Eric Dolphy* (IGDA, MILAN) p; **52tr** *Archie Shepp* (CHARLIE RECORDES LTD, LONDON) p; **53tl** *Sun Ra* (PHOTO GENNARO CILENTO) p; **53tc** *Malcolm X* (PHOTO EVE ARNOLD/MAGNUM/AGENZIA CONTRASTO, ROME) t; **53tr** *John Coltrane* (PHOTO VAL WILMER) t; **54l** *Jimi Hendrix* (PHOTO ROBERT KNIGHT/REDFERNS, LONDON) p; **55tr** *Miles Davis* (IGDA, MILAN) p; **56tl** *Anthony Braxton* (PHOTO STORYVILLE RECORDS) p; **56c** *Steve Lacy* (PHOTO PAOLA BENSI) p; **56b** *Art Ensemble of Chicago: Famoudoudon Moye* (PHOTO JOAN HACKETT) t; **57tr** *Henry Threadgill* (PHOTO JULES ALLEN) p; **58tl** Scene from the movie *The Cotton Club* by Francis Ford Coppola (ZOETROPE/ORION/THE KOBAL COLLECTION, LONDON) t; **58tr** *Keith Jarrett* (PHOTO ELENA CARMINATI) p; **59tl** *Pat Metheny* (PHOTO GUIDO HARARI/AGENZIA CONTRASTO, ROME) p; **60c** *Wynton Marsalis* (PHOTO ELENLA CARMLINATI) p; **60b** *Don Byron* (PHOTO ANTHONY BARBOZA) p; **61tc** *Joshua Redman* (PHOTO WEA) p; **61tr** *Steve Coleman* (PHOTO BMG) p.

COVER (clockwise from top left): **1.** *Skyline of New York* (IGDA-RIZZOLI, MILAN) p; **2.** 37tr; **3.** 31bl; **4.** 18bl; **5.** 16tl; **6.** 52tl; **7.** 22t; **8.** 41tl; **9.** 13tl; **10.** Illustration of John Coltrane; **11.** 52c; **12.** 41tc; **13.** 13t; **14.** 33tr; **15.** 18tl; **16.** 23tl; **17.** 58tr.

BACK COVER:
1. *Billie Holiday* (PHOTO WILLIAM GOTTLIEB/REDFERNS, LONDON) p.

CONTENTS

THE PROTAGONISTS

Jazz is a type of music that narrates the search for freedom. It surged in America at the turn of the century, when the descendants of African deported slaves faced the many facets of the New World's cultural life. In jazz, the many African heritages and the European musical culture of learned tradition, folk songs, and even military band music merged. It is an all-American art that developed its distinct and original language by expressing the emotions of the exiled African people. A worldwide phenomenon, the creative spark of jazz is still alive today.

♦ **A GOSPEL SINGER AND ROBERT JOHNSON** (1911–1938)
Religious songs and the blues— two protagonists of African-American music, inspired jazz.

♦ **ARRANGERS AND COMPOSERS**
Fletcher Henderson (1898–1952) and Jelly Roll Morton (1885–1941). Both pianists, they shaped the first jazz orchestral idiom.

♦ **BENNY GOODMAN** (1909–1986)
Clarinetist and bandleader. He was very popular in the 1930s and 1940s.

♦ **"COUNT" BASIE** (1904–1984)
Starting in the 1930s, he conducted a famous orchestra that was admired for its rhythm.

♦ **BILLIE HOLIDAY** (1915–1959)
The most acclaimed jazz singer of all time. Her voice is compared to that of a saxophone.

♦ **A SLAVE**
Slaves arrived in the United States in the eighteenth century and sang while they worked on plantations.

♦ **COLEMAN HAWKINS** (1901–1969)
One of the greatest virtuosos of the tenor saxophone, which he introduced to jazz.

♦ **LESTER YOUNG** (1909–1959)
First-class tenor saxophonist, he became popular in the mid-1930s.

♦ **THE REVOLUTIONARIES**
Charlie "Bird" Parker (1920–1955) and Dizzy Gillespie (1917–1993) Saxophonist and trumpeter, respectively. By the middle of the 1940s they were the forerunners of bebop.

♦ **GLENN MILLER** (1904–1944) With his orchestra, the most celebrated Big Band during World War II, he popularized jazz in Europe.

♦ **SONNY ROLLINS** (1930–) **AND CHARLES MINGUS** (1922–1979) One of the most talented saxophonists and double-bass player-composers.

♦ **MILES DAVIS** (1926–1991) Trumpeter and composer. The constant renovation of his music reflected his restless artistic progression.

♦ **JOHN "TRANE" COLTRANE** (1926–1967) Unsurpassed master of the saxophone, his music communicated a tormented spiritual quest.

♦ **ORNETTE COLEMAN** (1930–) A talented saxophonist, he was the free jazz theoretician that shook jazz in the 1960s.

♦ **HENRY THREADGILL** (1944–) Saxophonist and composer. He is considered the heir of Ellington and Mingus.

♦ **THELONIOUS MONK** (1917–1982) Pianist, composer, and one of the most restless geniuses of jazz.

♦ **CELEBRITIES** Duke Ellington (1899–1974) and Louis Armstrong (1901–1971). The most famous orchestra leader and trumpet player in the history of jazz.

♦ **STEVE COLEMAN** (1956–) Saxophonist, composer, and one of the new names in the world of jazz.

SLAVERY

In 1619, the first Africans were brought to Virginia. At first, they were employed as servants under contract in the English colonies; later, in the middle of the seventeenth century, the slave trade grew, receiving legislative recognition at the end of the century. Slaves were sold in auctions and bought mainly by planters to cultivate cotton, sugar, and coffee. Treated as property, slaves suffered great hardships and humiliations in the New World.

♦ FROM AFRICA TO AMERICA
Slave trade with Africa had started at the end of the fifteenth century when the Portuguese went in search of laborers for their colonies in the East Indies and in the New World. The Spanish, English, French, and Dutch followed them. Unscrupulous merchants, known as slave traders, bought people who were enslaved by other Africans during intertribal wars, exchanging them for goods, then stowing them in the holds of their ships. Chained in cramped, dark spaces, with little food and water, more than twelve million Africans during four centuries were forced to leave Africa and cross the Atlantic Ocean to reach the Americas after an excruciating two-month trip. Above, a watercolor portraying a French slave trade ship at the end of the seventeenth century.

♦ AN INHUMANE TRIP
Crowded into the ship, slaves started their odyssey. At least one and a half million of them died during the agonizing trip across the ocean. Above, an engraving showing the cruelty.

♦ DRAMATIC SCENES
Slaves had no rights. A mother could be separated from her children and each one could be sold separately.

♦ THE CIVIL WAR
Slavery was abolished in the United States in 1865, after the Civil War (left, a painting of a battle) was won by the Northern Abolitionist States over the South.

♦ SOLD AT AUCTION
After a period of quarantine following the hardships of their long voyage, slaves were sold in public auctions.

♦ THE AUCTIONEER
Paid by the slave traders, experienced auctioneers were in charge of selling the slaves.

♦ TEETH AND EYES
Plantation owners carefully checked the health status of the "property," especially the teeth and the whites of the eyes, for signs of illness.

THREE CENTURIES OF AFRO-AMERICA

Once they were bought by slave owners, the slaves were transferred to plantations or employed as house servants. In addition to large plantations, many small farms flourished in the South, where the white master often owned no more than one or two slaves. This caused the disintegration of social and family ties as well as the loss of cultural homogeneity among Africans, but it stressed contact with whites. And so a new culture was born, called African-American, which would later convey to music the complex story of the relationship between Africans and the New World.

♦ COTTON AND WHIPS

Cotton (above, in a 1787 engraving of a flower) was the most widely cultivated plant in the South. Thanks to the slaves, its production constantly increased. Production jumped from 80,000 tons in 1815 to 1,150,000 tons in 1861. Since the time needed to harvest cotton fibers was short, the slaves were forced to work nights by the light of the moon. Each slave was assigned a fixed quota of cotton to pick, which was regularly checked at the end of the day by weighing each basket. If the slave's workload was underweight, he or she was whipped. The wounds were later washed with water and salt to heal painfully and serve as a warning to the other slaves. Other products grown on the plantations were rice, sugar cane, tobacco, and hemp.

♦ THE WORK SONG

Following African custom, a leader sang and the other workers sang along, trying to catch the rhythm that would soothe them in their work. On the planatations, the first African-American musical form was born: the *Work Song*.

♦ THE BASKET

The slave carried a sack around his or her neck that emptied into a basket. Each slave picked almost 200 pounds (91 kg) of cotton in one day.

♦ **COTTON'S ROAD**
Once harvested, the cotton was prepared for shipment. At the end of the eighteenth century, with the first spinning machines, cotton ceased to be a luxury product.

♦ **MANSIONS AND SHACKS**
Near the master's lavish dwellings were the miserable slave quarters where the slaves were kept. Many had neither windows nor beds.

♦ **OVERSEERS WITH WHIPS**
The landowner or his overseers, who watched over the slaves, were ready to whip the slaves for the slightest offense.

SPIRITUALS

With its appealing messages of brotherhood and life after death, Christianity spread rapidly among the African slaves. In the church, they found the social and community acceptance that was elsewhere refused to them. Around the mid-eighteenth century, revived religious fervor and enthusiasm swept across America, converting many African-Americans. This new sensitivity gave birth to a new music, based on the poetic revelations of the Holy Scriptures. From then on, the African-American religious chant grew, characterized by its antiphonal structure (the call-and-response pattern between the preacher and the congregation), which was typical of African songs.

♦ **PRAISING THE LORD**
In the church, African-Americans stressed their own cultural identity with songs and dances. With the chants they confided their hopes and aspirations for a more dignified existence and for freedom.

♦ **THE RITUAL**
By 1820 there were almost 60,000 members of the Baptist Church. They found that the Christian rites and practices resembled the African customs of collective rituals that they were familiar with.

♦ **TRADITIONS**
Slave children approached music by listening and learning lyrics and tunes from their elders.

♦ BETWEEN THE
SACRED AND THE
PROFANE

Ancient religious
hymns from
Europe's most
diverse sources
are the origins of
the various forms
of early African-
American music,
upon which spiri-
tuals and gospel
music are based.
The spiritual is a
form of strongly
rhythmic folk and
collective song
dating from the
end of the eigh-
teenth century.
Gospel music is
a strong music
with a supple
structure and a
free rhythm that
would go onto
popularity outside
the church.
Together with
spirituals from
approximately the
mid-nineteenth
century, another
sound that
appealed enor-
mously to African-
Americans was
minstrel music.
Minstrel shows
featured white
actors with black
makeup who
imitated African-
American gestures
and attitudes.
African-American
minstrel troupes
(in the photo above)
were formed,
where African-
American actors
and singers pre-
sented shows with
European vaude-
ville components.

♦ DANCES
By 1816 church
segregation
allowed the
African com-
munity to
develop its
own music
and rituals,
culminating
in liberating
fast dances.

THE BLUES

The blues took shape at the end of the nineteenth century in the rural areas of the South, as a synthesis of more ancient forms of monodic or one-voice singing. Itinerant musicians, whose stage settings were village and city roads and small barrooms spread this music. The African-American blues musician expressed joys, sorrows, desires, and anxieties experienced along his road to acceptance into the white society after the abolition of slavery. The blues have an antiphonal structure, produced by alternating the voice and an impromptu musical theme.

♦ **ROBERT JOHNSON** (1911–1938) Guitar player and singer. He was one of the fathers of the Delta Blues, the typical blues heard around the Mississippi Delta. Between 1936 and 1937, he recorded 29 songs that have become classics. He suddenly disappeared under mysterious circumstances.

♦ **THE SHACKS**
African-American families lived in humble shacks in abject poverty.

♦ **MUSIC AND LIFE**
The blues music narrates everyday true personal experiences with realistic—and often humorous—tones.

♦ **THE MUSIC**
Precursor of jazz, this timeless and outstanding music continues today to renew its forms of expression. In the 1940s and 1950s, the popularity of the blues surpassed that of jazz.

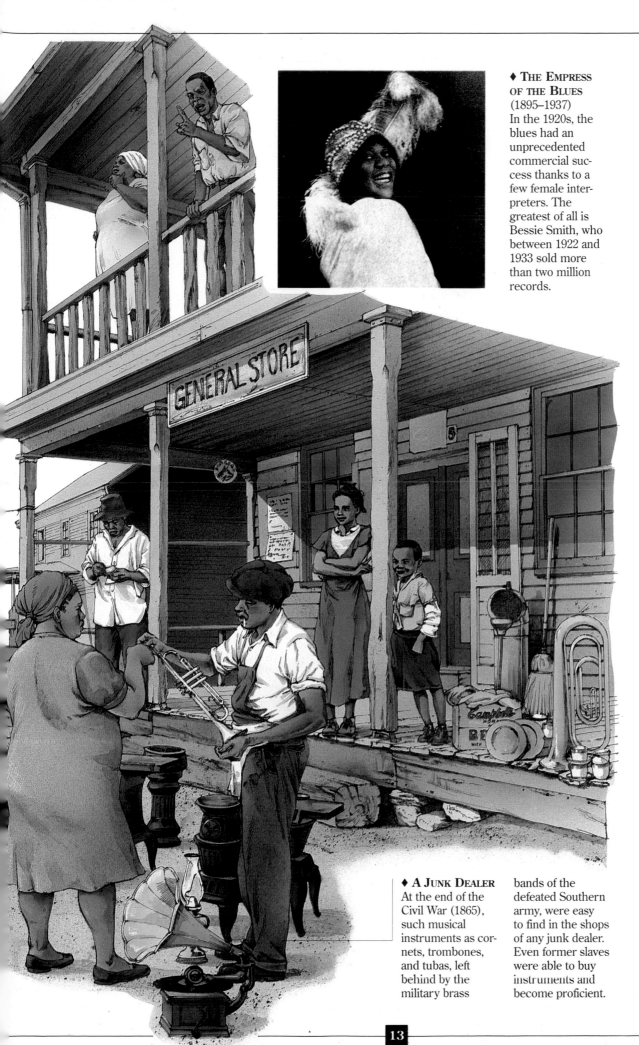

♦ THE EMPRESS OF THE BLUES
(1895–1937)
In the 1920s, the blues had an unprecedented commercial success thanks to a few female interpreters. The greatest of all is Bessie Smith, who between 1922 and 1933 sold more than two million records.

♦ RAGTIME
At the end of the nineteenth century, another musical style, an ancestor of jazz, flourished. It was called ragtime, a lively and rhythmic music originally composed for piano. Ragtime is formed by the two words *rag* and *time,* suggestive of the typical syncopated rhythm marked by constant acceleration. From piano music performed on perforated player piano rolls, ragtime turned into an orchestral music. Its most noteworthy representative was Scott Joplin (1868–1917), composer of the famous "Maple Leaf Rag" (above, an original sheet of music). Ragtime, also popular in Europe, inspired the first jazz piano soloists such as James P. Johnson (1894–1955), Fats Waller (1904–1943), Willie "The Lion" Smith (1897–1973), and "Jelly Roll" Morton (1885–1941).

♦ A JUNK DEALER
At the end of the Civil War (1865), such musical instruments as cornets, trombones, and tubas, left behind by the military brass bands of the defeated Southern army, were easy to find in the shops of any junk dealer. Even former slaves were able to buy instruments and become proficient.

NEW ORLEANS

At the end of the nineteenth century, the new musical style, called jazz from then on, found its home in New Orleans. In the 1920s, this music would be referred to as Dixieland. The first New Orleans bands were brass bands, ensembles containing cornets, trombones, and tubas played by six or seven musicians. The typical style of New Orleans jazz is based on polyphony—the soloists simultaneously play distinct melodies—and on collective improvisation, where each instrumentalist creates his part on the spot taking inspiration from the theme of the piece as enunciated by the main soloist. Musicians, in turn, perform ad-lib brief solos called breaks.

♦ JOE "KING" OLIVER (1885–1938) Cornetist, composer, and one of the early prominent figures of New Orleans jazz. Between 1922 and 1924, Louis Armstrong was second cornet in his band.

♦ ALONG THE MISSISSIPPI
A typical riverboat of the South shown in a colored lithograph of the time. On board, the first jazz bands played their tunes, spreading the new music.

♦ BARBER IN THE DAYTIME, CORNETIST AT NIGHT
Charles "Buddy" Bolden (1877–1931), legendary virtuoso of the cornet of the early jazz era, was a barber. The sound of his cornet was said to be so powerful that it could be heard 12 miles away. There are no recordings in existence today of his music.

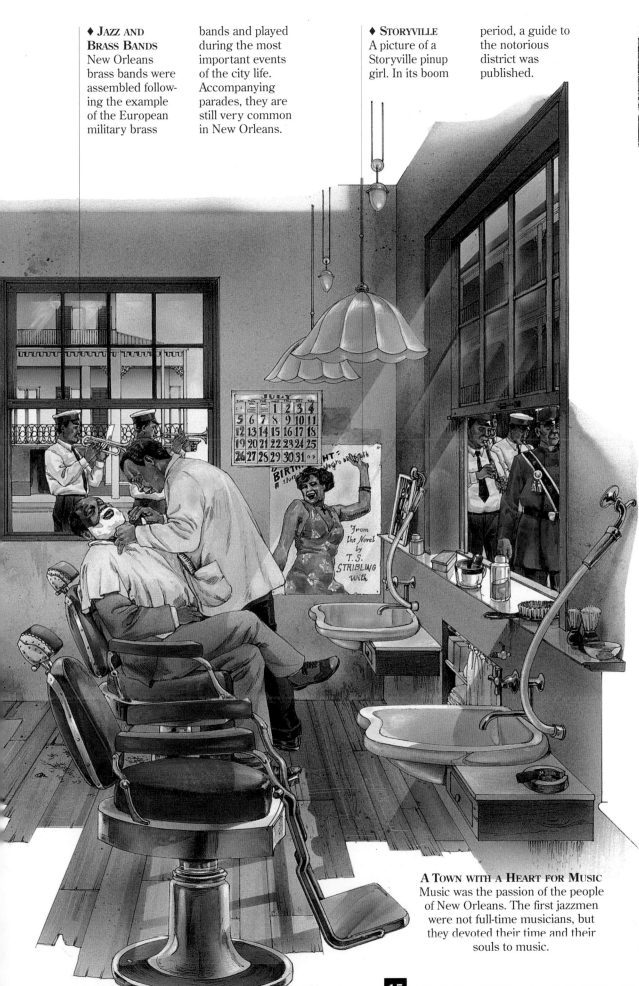

♦ **JAZZ AND BRASS BANDS**
New Orleans brass bands were assembled following the example of the European military brass bands and played during the most important events of the city life. Accompanying parades, they are still very common in New Orleans.

♦ **STORYVILLE**
A picture of a Storyville pinup girl. In its boom period, a guide to the notorious district was published.

♦ **THE CAPITAL OF MUSIC**
First the French, then the Spanish dominated New Orleans. In 1803 Napoleon sold the territory to the United States in the Louisiana Purchase. This explains the city's mixture of different cultures and ethnic elements evident in the architecture of The French Quarter. Music is everywhere in New Orleans, and brass bands are a familiar presence at parties and picnics along the banks of the Mississippi River, as well as at weddings and funerals. The most important jazz district, however, was Storyville (shown above in an early twentieth-century lithograph), created in 1897. Its night-life sparkled with entertainment and illegal businesses. Several cabarets hosted women of pleasure and employed the first jazz musicians with their lively, captivating music. Storyville was closed in 1917 and the New Orleans jazz musicians emigrated to the North carrying their music with them.

A TOWN WITH A HEART FOR MUSIC
Music was the passion of the people of New Orleans. The first jazzmen were not full-time musicians, but they devoted their time and their souls to music.

LOUIS ARMSTRONG

"Satchmo" was one of the greatest jazz soloists of all time, the musician who defined some of the characteristics of jazz that remain today. Thanks to him, the solo—a series of variations executed by the musician on the melody chosen as the point of departure of the music—became the heart of the performance. The wonderful sound of his trumpet, almost an extension of his voice, was vigorous, dramatic, and uniquely magic. After him, every jazz musician would search for his own sound. Extraordinary showman, he was, above all, the world's ambassador of jazz, an artist gifted with an irresistible verve and jovial empathy, loved by his audiences.

♦ **LOUIS ARMSTRONG** (1901–1971) In his hometown, New Orleans, the young Louis Armstrong had his musical debut in a vocal quartet formed with some friends. He mastered the cornet and in the 1920s accompanied the most popular blues singers, like Bessie Smith, becoming known as a second trumpet in King Oliver's Creole Jazz Band. His hits as a soloist were composed around the middle of the 1920s with his bands, the Hot Fives and the Hot Seven, with whom he created such great successes as: "West End Blues," "Potato Head Blues," "St. James Infirmary," and "Cornet Chop Suey." His long and versatile career was marked by a steady success and lasted until the 1960s. In 1952 the readers of the music magazine *Down Beat* elected him "the most important musician of all time."

♦ **BASEBALL AND MUSIC** The favorite pastime of Louis' friends was sports. In the reform school, the young men participated in sports, played music, and were made to choose jobs.

♦ **A SHOT IN STORYVILLE**
In 1912 a gun was fired on New Year's Eve and eleven-year-old Louis Armstrong was sent to prison, a reform school, the Colored Waifs' Home for Boys. It is here, that his musical career began, in the Waifs' Home Brass Band.

♦ **BIX BEIDERBECKE**
(1903–1931)
Beiderbecke had a wretched life. An outstanding cornetist, his introverted style counteracted that of Armstrong. He died young, destroyed by alcohol.

♦ **A MUSIC TEACHER**
Peter Davis, who directed the Waifs' Home Brass Band, gave Louis Armstrong his first music lessons. He trained him first on the tambourine, then on the saxophone, and finally on the cornet.

THE ORGANIZATION OF JAZZ

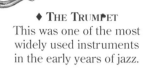

With the closing of Storyville in 1917, the migration of musicians from New Orleans spread the sound of jazz from coast to coast. Its original simple sound was later replaced by a more complex relationship between the soloist and the ensemble. By the middle of the 1920s, big bands, ten-piece and larger orchestras, appeared on the musical scene. The repertory started to be based on more and more elaborate arrangements, thanks to the creations of such musicians as pianist Jelly Roll Morton and composer Fletcher Henderson. The rhythm of jazz became smoother and the steady movement called swing, which represents one of the elements of jazz, emerged.

♦ **FERDINAND "JELLY ROLL" MORTON**
(1885–1941)
Pianist, singer, and composer, Jelly Roll Morton remains one of the most picturesque jazz figures. Of Creole background, a descendant of Africans and French, he grew up in New Orleans where he began his career playing the piano in Storyville's clubs. He had the gift for fine arrangements. From his music, a unique cross of jazz and Latin American rhythms emerged, the sound of vibrant New Orleans. Heading a group named the Red Hot Peppers, he recorded a series of well-known songs and extensively toured the United States, presenting himself as the father of jazz. Below, a detail of the cover of one of his earliest editions.

♦ **THE TRUMPET**
This was one of the most widely used instruments in the early years of jazz.

♦ **THE SCORES**
The increasing popularity of jazz relied on the new professional jazz soloists' ability to read music.

♦ **THE BASS TUBA**
This was used in rhythmic function alternating with the double bass, which would eventually take its place in the 1930s.

♦ **THE BANDLEADER**
Seated at the piano, Fletcher Henderson trained and conducted his musicians.

♦ THE CLARINET
One of the instruments that characterized early jazz, which would later fade.

♦ THE SLIDE TROMBONE
From its raw and deep New Orleans sounds, following the development of jazz, it acquired articulation and rhythmic smoothness.

♦ THE SAXOPHONES
Used in military brass bands, saxophones occupied a place of primary importance among jazz instruments.

♦ THE BIG BAND IN CONCERT
Dressed in striking, elegant suits, often in tuxedos, the musicians in early jazz orchestras were cheered by audiences in the country's nightclubs and dance halls.

♦ FLETCHER HENDERSON
(1898–1952)
He started his career as both a pianist and an accompanist of blues singers, but his role, from the 1920s on, was that of orchestra leader. He was known above all as an arranger, being one of the first innovators to conceive a specific musical structure for each single piece. In New York, Henderson defined, with Don Redman, the basic principles of the jazz orchestral idiom. Their scores channel the New Orleans polyphony, assigning the roles of each instrument to the various orchestral sections: saxophones, clarinets, trumpets, and trombones. Henderson perfected many devices such as the head arrangement, devised on the spur of the moment and constructed through riffs—brief phrases played repetitively,—which were able to create a background to accompany the soloist.

♦ THE MARK OF THE ORCHESTRA
The bandleader's initials were marked on each musician's music stands.

♦ THE MUTES
Made of aluminum, rubber, and polystyrene, they can be fitted into the trumpet and trombone's bell, producing effects similar to the human voice.

THE CITIES

The 1920s were called the Roaring Twenties. The era, raised to literary fame by the novels of F. Scott Fitzgerald, was marked by a wild gusto for life that ended with the stock market crash in 1929. These were the Prohibition years, during which the manufacture and sale of alcoholic beverages were forbidden and gangsters lived well from their illegal activities. Nightlife revolved around parties, movies and theaters, and, later in the evening, in clandestine nightclubs and bars called "speakeasies," where it was possible to buy smuggled alcohol. Every city was vibrantly alive and their soundtracks were the frenzied rhythm of jazz. The new music spread in this way from suburban slums to upscale neighborhoods.

♦ **THE SUPERSTARS** Movie stars arrived at the theater for the preview of their film, which had already entered into the new era of talking pictures.

♦ **IN SEARCH OF AUTOGRAPHS** Crowds of fans gathered outside the movie theater in the hope of seeing their favorite stars and getting their autographs.

♦ **NO MORE WHISKY** With the Volstead Act of 1920, the manufacture and use of alcohol was forbidden, until its repeal on December 5, 1933. On the left, alcoholic beverages confiscated in a "speakeasy" in 1923.

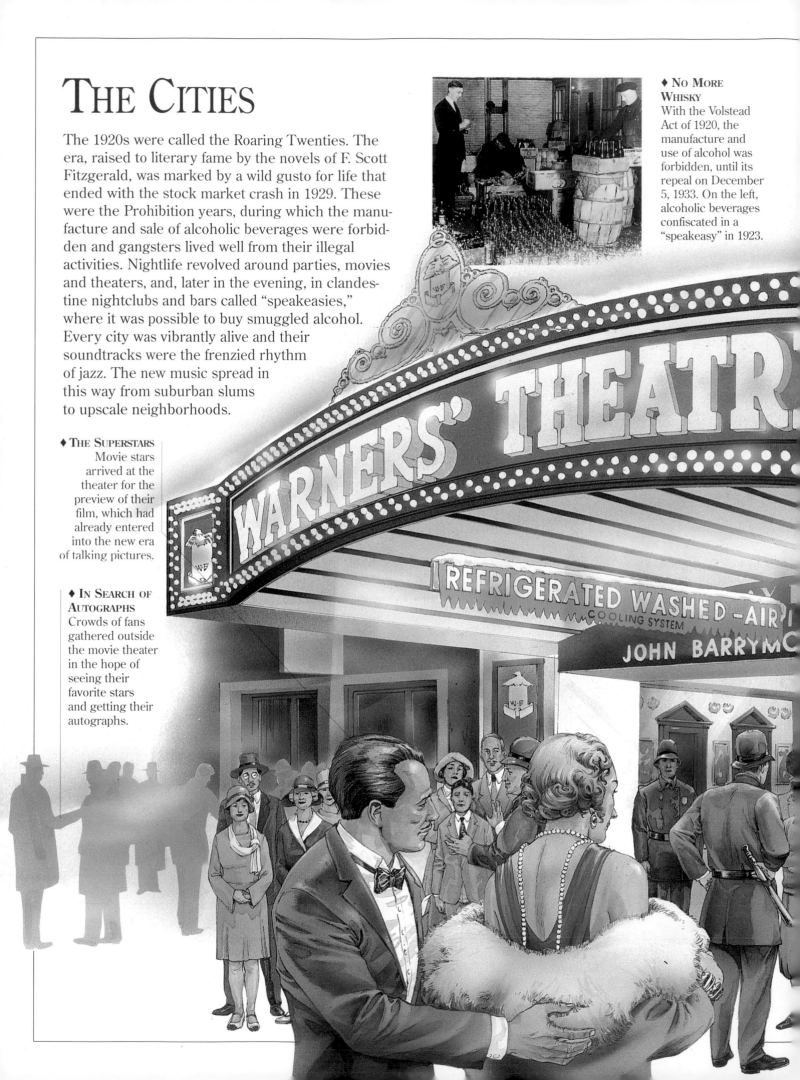

♦ TALKING PICTURES
A big crowd waited for the premiere
of *Don Juan* by Warner Brothers,
one of the first talking pictures.
The movie company had purchased
the Piccadilly Theater in New York
City, reopening it under the name
of Warner's Theatre. Its first production
was *Don Juan* in August 1926.

♦ GEORGE GERSHWIN
(1898–1937)
One of the best-known American
composers, Gershwin took the
inspiration for his music from
jazz. Among his jazz-related
hits is the famous *Rhapsody
in Blue,* performed in New
York City in 1924. Many
pieces by Gershwin are
now considered jazz.

♦ F. SCOTT FITZGERALD
(1896–1940)
The novelist described the America of the
1920s and created such memorable characters as the unscrupulous adventurer
who was the protagonist of his most
famous book, *The Great Gatsby* (1925).

HARLEM

During the 1920s Harlem, in upper Manhattan, became the cultural magnet of African-Americans. It was the center of convergence of the hopes of their emancipation and progress, especially after the enlistment of African-Americans into the armed services during World War I. This period was enlightened not only by musicians, but also by writers, poets, and painters, and was known as the "Harlem Renaissance," in homage to its new artistic and political sensitivity. The dynamism of this district soon attracted white intellectuals as well. Theaters and nightclubs rapidly opened, where such influential jazz artists as Duke Ellington, Cab Calloway, and Fats Waller regularly performed.

♦ **A GANGSTER FOR A MANAGER**
Located on the corner between Lenox Avenue and 142nd Street, the Cotton Club (on the left in a photograph from that era) was opened by the New York gangster, Owney Madden, in 1923.

♦ **MYSTERY AND FASCINATION**
One of the most famous nightspots was the Cotton Club, whose shows lured flocks of people thanks to a strong sensual attraction that came from the combination of music and dance. Its name was adapted from African-American roots—the cotton fields.

♦ **A FRENZIED RHYTHM**
In Harlem, tap dancers fascinated audiences. Their agile, acrobatic dancing was backed up by a stepping rhythm produced by small metallic plates placed on the bottom of their shoes.

♦ **WHITE AUDIENCE ONLY**
A selected white clientele, including movie stars and other celebrities, frequented the major Harlem clubs. African-Americans were not allowed in.

♦ CAB CALLOWAY
(1907–1994)
Calloway and his band replaced Ellington at the Cotton Club. His hits were a parody of African-American ghetto characters.

♦ THOMAS W. "FATS" WALLER
(1904–1943)
A pianist, a singer, and a composer, he was one of the protagonists of the Harlem Renaissance. As a piano soloist, he was the father of the *stride* style, a left-hand bass pattern and an elaboration of the ragtime rhythmical structure.

♦ DUKE ELLINGTON
(1899–1974)
Nicknamed "Duke" for his refined elegance and class, he became the top attraction in Harlem at the Cotton Club, where he and his band played from 1927 to 1931. His music is perhaps the most complete of the African-American tradition. It is a synthesis of African ancestral memories and European composition. Ellington composed his pieces with his individual soloist's instrumental skills in mind. After World War II, he focused on writing ambitious compositions that were characterized by an extended and complex structure. He remained active with his orchestra until his death, with a succession of successes. Among his hits are: "Mood Indigo" (1930), "Sophisticated Lady" (1933), and "Take the A Train" (1937).

♦ A NIGHT IN THE JUNGLE
The music of Ellington's band was called "jungle music" for its unusual sound effects and the mysterious atmosphere evoked by his trumpets and muted trombones.

JAZZ IN EUROPE

By the 1920s, the first American musicians had arrived in Europe. Enthusiastic crowds were waiting for them in London, Berlin, and, above all, Paris, which demonstrated its sophistication by devoting an attention to jazz that it had previously reserved only for African art. At the beginning of the twentieth century, the so-called primitive art had been the inspiration for figurative arts innovators. Then, jazz attracted attention with the same blend of mystery and exoticism, perfectly embodied in famed entertainer Josephine Baker. A singer and dancer from the Cotton Club, she arrived in Paris in 1925 with the show "Revue Nègre," accompanied by a group of musicians, including the great saxophonist Sidney Bechet.

♦ **FROM AFRICA TO THE WORLD VIA PARIS**
Charles Ratton's studio displayed an exclusive selection of African objects. Museums called on him for the most important exhibits of the time on the subject. In 1933 Ratton contributed one hundred pieces to the "All African" exhibit in Chicago.

♦ **PRECIOUS OBJECTS**
It was possible to find in the studio very ancient, small ivory statuettes of every size and origin.

♦ **DJANGO REINHARDT** (1910–1953)
A guitarist of gypsy origin, he was among the first to find, in the 1930s, a European channel to jazz, adapting swing to the music of his people.

♦ **SIDNEY BECHET**
(1897–1959)
A talented
clarinetist and
a soprano saxo-
phonist, Sidney
Bechet (above) is
one of the most
distinctive figures
of jazz, known for
his strong vibrato
and his deep
sense of the blues.
After starting in
New Orleans, he
was one of the
first jazz musi-
cians to land in
Europe (in
London, in 1922).
He traveled back
and forth between
Europe and the
United States, and
in 1949 he moved
permanently to
France, where
he worked with
several French
musicians. He was
so popular that
the whole town of
Antibes celebrated
his wedding in
1951. In France
he was awarded a
gold record for
the extraordinary
success of his
recording "Petit
Fleur." A soloist
of the same
caliber as Louis
Armstrong, he
recorded such
hits as "Blues
in Thirds"
(1938) and
"Summertime"
(1939).

♦ **THE REVUE
NÈGRE**
Already a star at
Harlem's Cotton
Club, Josephine
Baker (1906–1975)
took Paris by
storm with her
sensual dances.

♦ **TREASURES
FROM OTHER
COUNTRIES**
Works of art were
carefully packed
up to be sent to
exhibits in other
countries.

JAM SESSIONS

In the economically depressed 1930s, Kansas City became the main experimental laboratory of jazz. Soloists of the most important bands gathered at night, after work, in small, smoky nightclubs to duel in jam sessions, which soon became one of jazz's most typical formulas. These artists improvised on a single song, a blues tune, or a simple harmonic progression. The musicians, not limited in their performances by time or contract, were free to try anything, constantly challenging each other in a mutually rewarding exchange.

♦ **COUNT BASIE** (1904-1984) William Basie, nicknamed "Count," was the most prominent figure in Kansas City jazz. He was a pianist, composer, arranger, and leader of one of the most influential jazz bands.

♦ **THE JAM AUDIENCE** Only a few people—friends of the musicians— were privileged enough to attend the jam sessions.

♦ **POLITICIANS AND GANGSTERS** In Kansas City a corrupt administration accommodated the business of cabarets and nightclubs that were run by gangsters. Among the most famous clubs were: the Sunset, the Lonestar, the Subway, and the Cherry Blossom.

♦ **LESTER YOUNG** (1909–1959) A virtuoso of the tenor sax with a relaxed musical style and a light sound, he was a mentor for other jazz musicians until the 1950s.

♦ **ROY ELDRIDGE** (1911–1989) He was the trumpeter at the front of numerous jam sessions, known for his explosive style that was influenced by Louis Armstrong.

♦ **THE BATTLE OF THE BANDS** In the scorching atmosphere of the jam sessions, instrumental battles, such as the "saxophone battles," took place. Every saxophonist picked up the solo from the last musical phrase played by the previous soloist, and so on.

♦ **JAZZ AT THE PHILHARMONIC** In 1944 the impresario and record producer, Norman Granz (1918), decided to introduce the jam session idea to the general public. He assembled a few famous jazz musicians for the first "Jazz at the Philharmonic," so named because it took place at the Philharmonic Auditorium in Los Angeles. The show was a hit and Granz went on to use this same formula in international tours across Europe, Japan, and Australia until 1967.

♦ **POKER AND GUNS** In one of the private rooms, the manager and some friends played cards.

♦ **LATE AT NIGHT** Clean up time at the club. It was common for musicians to play until dawn.

♦ **ART TATUM** (1910–1956) Certain artists dominated the jam sessions because of their supreme technical skills. One of these was pianist Art Tatum, a definitive jazz virtuoso.

JAZZ IN THEATERS

At the end of the 1930s, after nightclubs and cabarets had opened their doors to jazz, such theaters as the prestigious Carnegie Hall, which usually hosted performances of ballet and classical music, welcomed it. It was a glorious moment for jazz as its artistic dignity was asserted nationally after its early years as ballroom and entertainment music. This new dimension of jazz continued to gain ground. From the postwar years to the present time, it has become common to listen to jazz performances in concert halls.

♦ **A ROUND OF SWING**
The program featured performances by the Benny Goodman Trio, Quartet, and then Orchestra, and such celebrities as Count Basie and Lester Young.

♦ **SOLD OUT!**
A huge crowd occupied every seat and it was necessary to bring extra chairs on stage to accommodate the audience.

♦ **BLACKS AND WHITES TOGETHER ON STAGE**
In Benny Goodman's Quartet, there are two African-American musicians: Lionel Hampton on vibes and Teddy Wilson on piano, as well as the white Gene Krupa on drums.

28

♦ **A HISTORIC EVENT**
On January 16, 1938, jazz arrived at Carnegie Hall in New York City. On stage were blues and gospel singers and such famous jazz musicians as Benny Goodman. This was a memorable event that celebrated the origin and the development of jazz.

♦ **BENNY GOODMAN**
(1909–1986)
Clarinetist, saxophonist, and bandleader, he began his musical career at eleven, joining many groups in his hometown of Chicago at a very young age. In 1932 he formed his first group, which by 1935 became one of the most famous of all swing bands. At the clarinet, Goodman had a clear sound and a fluid phrasing that enhanced the rhythm of swing. For this reason, the public crowned him "The King of Swing." He played with small bands that were greatly appreciated for their refined performances. He toured Asia and Europe with his band, becoming one of the ambassadors of jazz. Brilliant arrangers such as Fletcher Henderson and a renowned group of soloists contributed to his success. His humble origins as the son of a poor tailor and his successes were told in a 1955 movie, *The Benny Goodman Story.*

♦ **CARNEGIE HALL**
Inaugurated on May 5, 1891, Tchaikovsky and Toscanini performed here as conductors, and the New York Philharmonic Orchestra has long established its reputation here. The room seated 2,760 (above, in an engraving).

DRUMS

Drums are the musical instruments that most characterize jazz. Made by assembling different percussion instruments, they incorporate ancient African sounds and the military drums of European brass bands. According to tradition, in 1895, DeeDee Chandler, a New Orleans musician, attached a foot pedal to the bass drum so that it was possible for the musician to play both cymbals and drums. Drums became the symbol of the extraordinary rhythmic richness and complexity of this music. The evolution of their sound accompanies the transformations of jazz, from the rigid rhythmic beat at the beginning, to the agility of swing, to the violent rhythms of free jazz in the 1960s.

♦ **TOM-TOM**
Placed on top or beside the bass drum, these are drums that clearly have African origins.

♦ **HI-HAT CYMBALS**
Introduced around the middle of the 1920s, these are formed by placing two cymbals on top of each other and clashing them together by means of a foot pedal, producing a short or long sound. The difference in sound is obtained when the two cymbals are either together or separated.

♦ **THE BASS DRUM**
A large drum with a deep sound. This drum comes equipped with a foot pedal, which marks the beat.

♦ **THE SNARE DRUM**
Typical of military bands, the snare drum, also known as the side drum, produces its sound thanks to a series of steel strings stretched underneath the drum.

♦ **BABY DODDS**
(1898–1959)
One of the heros of early jazz, his style exploited different drum sounds.

♦ **CYMBALS**
Made of a copper alloy, cymbals vary in size. The large ones are called "ride" and are used to keep the beat. The small ones are the "crash" and the "splash" and produce the various rhythmic accents.

♦ **STICKS AND WIRE BRUSHES**
Drums are played with sticks and mallets, as well as wire brushes, which are used to produce a more muffled sound. In the picture at the right, note the position of the sticks in the hands of a jazz drummer.

♦ **KENNY CLARKE**
(1914–1985)
Protagonist of bop drums, he was the first to use the ride cymbal instead of the Charleston cymbal to keep the beat. Drums did not simply maintain the beat for him, they combined with the other instruments. He was a member of the original Modern Jazz Quartet. In 1956 he moved to Paris.

♦ **SKINS**
Originally, drumheads were made from animal skins, but since the 1960s, they have been made with synthetic material. The skins are turned by adjusting a series of taps.

♦ **ELVIN JONES**
(1927–)
He is pure force and energy on drums. His style, developed in the 1960s in John Coltrane's band, reflects the complexity of African music, which he reproduces by creating a compact rhythmic texture, which with a whirlwind quality, carries the soloists.

♦ **JO JONES**
(1911–1985)
Master of swing, he improved on the use of the Charleston (hi-hat) cymbal to create a light and airy rhythm.

A MUSICAL JOURNEY

The standards, a huge repertory of popular songs, often taken from musicals and jazz pieces, represent an important source of inspiration for jazz. Standards have always served jazz musicians well and are revamped with every new interpretation. For instance, the song "Body and Soul" has been a standard for saxophonists since its historical version by Coleman Hawkins in 1939. Its various interpretations illustrate the changes in jazz.

♦ **COLEMAN HAWKINS** (1901–1969) In the 1920s Hawkins invented the use of the tenor sax as a major solo instrument. His "Body and Soul" remains unsurpassed. It is a monologue that poetically reinvents the piece by exploiting its harmonic and melodic resources.

♦ **SONNY ROLLINS** (1930–) He recorded "Body and Soul" in 1958. His version for solo saxophone benefitted from Hawkins' influence, which continues to inspire modern jazz compositions.

♦ **BENNY CARTER** (1907–) In 1961 the respected saxophonist, arranger, and composer Benny Carter revived Hawkins' "Body and Soul."

♦ **THE KING OF THE SAXOPHONE**
"Don't you know he was the King of Saxophone, yes indeed he was. Talkin' 'bout the guy that made it sound so good. Some people knew him by 'the Bean,' but Hawkins was his name. He sure could swing…" So sings Eddie Jefferson, who wrote these lyrics for the famous Hawkins' solo, some of the notes of which are shown here.

♦ **CASSANDRA WILSON**
(1955–)
One of the most popular jazz singers today. In 1990 she performed her own version of "Body and Soul," in which John Coltrane's arrangement and non-jazz musical background are noticeable.

♦ **JOHN "TRANE" COLTRANE**
(1926–1967)
In the 1960s, his interpretation of "Body and Soul" was a breakthrough. Coltrane changed the original rhythm to offer a faster version of the classic. It was much different from the Hawkins' lyrical and soft version.

♦ **EDDIE JEFFERSON**
(1918–1979)
Singer and poet, he was an expert at "vocalese," the technique he used to interpret the most famous jazz solos, substituting words for notes. His 1976 version of Coleman Hawkins' "Body and Soul" is an example.

33

THE VOICES OF JAZZ

In the 1930s, big bands played on the jazz scene. They featured one or more vocalists, each with a definite style. The jazz vocalist has always been a soloist, just as the other musicians with whom the vocalist shared tone coloration and rhythmic, melodic, and harmonic freedom. The singer continuously carries on a dialogue with the band instrumentalists, always in search of improvisational cues and offering inspiration in return for new musical inventions.

♦ BILLIE "LADY DAY" HOLIDAY
(1915–1959)
Billie Holiday was only sixteen when she started her career in Benny Goodman's band and became one of the first ladies of jazz. She collaborated with the greatest musicians of the 1930s and 1940s, and, in particular, with Count Basie and Lester Young, with whom she recorded many hits. Her life was marred by tragedy, ranging from racism to imprisonment and from alcohol abuse to drug addiction. Perhaps this is the reason why Billie Holiday interpreted the feelings portrayed in her songs so emotionally. Her singing, clean and free of embellishments, was enhanced by a perfect sense of rhythm, which allowed her to relate to the other instrumentalists. She recounted her life in her autobiography, *Lady Sings the Blues,* which also inspired a movie. Among her most famous recordings are "Strange Fruit" (1939) and "Don't Explain" (1945).

♦ CARMEN McRAE
(1922–1994)
One of Billie Holiday's followers, her singing, strongly influenced by the blues, was pure and elegant.

♦ ELLA FITZGERALD
(1918–1996)
She won a talent contest in 1934 and was an extraordinarily talented singer, known for her scat improvising and vocal clarity.

♦ SARAH VAUGHAN
(1924–1990)
Acclaimed in the 1940s, she was a voice virtuoso, known for her phrasing and versatility.

♦ DINAH WASHINGTON
(1924–1963)
Faithful to the blues and gospel traditions, she enjoyed enormous popularity with African-American audiences.

♦ JIMMY RUSHING
(1903–1972)
With his powerful voice, linked to the blues tradition, Rushing was the symbol of Kansas City jazz.

♦ FRANK SINATRA
(1915–1998)
After starting with Harry James' orchestra, Sinatra established his reputation in 1940 with Tommy Dorsey and became one of the most popular entertainers of the twentieth century.

♦ SCAT SINGING
Scat is a style of jazz singing in which a singer uses nonsense syllables, often onomatopoeic, to create musical phrases and improvise on the original theme.
The origins of scat date back to New Orleans jazz. The first artist to raise it to the level of musical art was Louis Armstrong (above), a singer as well as a trumpeter, who used it in 1926 when he recorded "Heebie Jeebies." Ella Fitzgerald, an extraordinary jazz singer, was a daring scat improviser.
Cab Calloway frequently used it at the Cotton Club, involving the audience in repeating some of his classic nonsense words such as *zaz, zuh,* and *za* in time to his rhythm. Scat singing is still alive today, used by many contemporary artists. Among them is Bobby McFerrin (1950–), who was very popular in the 1980s.

♦ BILLIE'S
LESSON
Billie Holiday's concerts attracted many celebrities, not only musicians, who were fascinated by her enormous talent.

JAZZ DURING WWII

By the early 1940s, during World War II, jazz was regarded as a symbol of solidarity and hope for American soldiers. Both the U.S. Army and Navy promoted the formation of military big bands (where many jazz artists would first train), which followed the troops. Even those illustrious musicians left at home contributed with the recordings of V-Discs, produced exclusively for the Army. Broadcast via radio or performed live, jazz gained new fans in the countries liberated by Allied troops.

♦ **GLENN MILLER**
(1904–1944)
An extremely popular trombone player and bandleader, he was also director of the Air Force Orchestra. He was killed in a plane crash while flying to Paris for a concert. Above, he is shown with some musicians in Great Britain.

♦ **THE SOUND OF AN ERA**
Glenn Miller's music led the way to the Big Band Era, thanks to popular songs like "In the Mood," "Little Brown Jug," and other classics.

♦ **JAZZ IN A LIBERATED EUROPE**
American troops liberated European towns. At first opposed by totalitarian leaders, jazz started to spread thanks to the V-Discs that American soldiers carried with them.

♦ **V-DISCS**
Short for Victory Discs, they were produced from 1942 to 1948 and conceived by the U.S. Department of War for use by the soldiers involved in the conflict. They document various types of music: classical, pop, and jazz. Jazz recordings become important when, from 1942 to 1944, musicians decided to go on strike to get more money for their recording services. V-Discs contained the unique recordings of the time of Duke Ellington, Billie Holiday, and other popular artists. In 1949 the original recordings were destroyed and V-Discs became precious collectors' items. Recently, many V-Discs have been rerecorded on compact disks (CDs). Above, a V-Disc label.

♦ **ON THE WINGS OF AN AIRPLANE**
In a hangar that was transformed into a concert hall, airplanes were used as theater boxes to watch the show.

♦ **SWING AND BOMBERS**
A concert in an airplane hangar became a festive event and a way to temporarily forget the horrors of war.

BEBOP

♦ CHARLIE "BIRD" PARKER (1920–1955) Saxophonist Parker's career started in the band of Jay McShann in his hometown of Kansas City at the end of the 1930s. In 1941 he moved to New York where he became a part of the jam sessions at Minton's Playhouse and The Village Vanguard, the birthplaces of bebop. He was the most exciting soloist of the new music. Some of his critics claimed that his tense and tormented style would kill jazz, but his harmonic and melodic innovations gave birth to postwar jazz. He played with Dizzy Gillespie, Bud Powell, and the young trumpeter, Miles Davis. He even recorded historical cuts with a violin ensemble. The dramatic intensity of his solos reflected his personal battles with drugs and alcohol that he would eventually lose while still young.

In the middle of the 1940s, jazz went through an important change. While the bands of the time played dance and entertainment music, some musicians sought freedom of expression and independence from the limitations of show business. Applying the ideas developed during their jam sessions, a revolution suddenly exploded in New York. This eruption was bebop, modern jazz, which lifted the figure of the jazz performer to artistic heights and extended the role of the improviser from the soloist to the other band members. Dry and fast-paced, with unusual breaks, bebop conquered the convulsive spirit of urban America. The demanding harmonic and rhythmic complexity of this music required extraordinary instrumental skills.

♦ CHARLIE CHRISTIAN (1916–1942) One of the first musicians to adopt the electric guitar, with his single note solos he was one of the founders of bebop.

♦ COMBOS Big bands were replaced by five- or six-piece small bands called combos.

♦ JAZZ AS A MUSICAL ART FORM With bebop, jazz turned into a type of music that required careful listening. The jazz club became the host of the new music, which had enthusiastic supporters.

♦ A BARONESS FASCINATED BY JAZZ Intellectuals and benefactors loved bebop, among them, the Baroness Nica de Konigswater.

♦ THE JAZZ FAN Devoted jazz fans recorded the concerts of their idols. Those recordings would be issued in later years.

♦ **DIZZY GILLESPIE** (1917–1993) Nicknamed "Dizzy" for his ebullient and extroverted character, John Birks Gillespie began his career in Teddy Hill's band and later in Cab Calloway's band, before moving on as a soloist. His exuberant personality ensured him the success his friend and colleague, Charlie Parker, never had. He performed with him in a number of small bands while continuing to enthusiastically conduct his own big band for many years. At the end of the 1940s, he adopted Latin American rhythms after the addition to his band of the Cuban drummer, Chano Pozo. He also experimented with scat. In 1952 he adopted his trademark bent-bell trumpet, with its upturned bell on which he projects his spectacular style. He left an important legacy to the world of bop.

♦ **SPECIAL SURVEILLANCE** Because of their reputation for being rebellious, the musicians were often checked by police.

♦ **BEBOP STREET** The clubs on 52nd Street in New York gave the street the new bebop address.

♦ **BUD POWELL** (1924–1966) Talented but tortured pianist, composer, and arranger. With his great technique and his innovative style, he was, along with Charlie Parker and Dizzy Gillespie, one of the originators of bebop.

RHYTHM AND BLUES

During the 1940s many African-Americans moved from the rural areas of the South to the big cities of the North to work in the defense plants. Their music followed the tradition of gospel and blues songs, which, crossing paths with big band swing, created rhythm and blues. The focal point of this rhythmically swaying new music was singing, and soloists were also able to extract sounds from their instruments similar to human cries.

♦ **THE SON OF RHYTHM AND BLUES—ROCK AND ROLL**
From the blues and rhythm and blues came the sensual and energetic force that would become rock and roll, as well as a preference for a marked rhythmic pulsation and the use of the electric guitar. The term "rock and roll" can be heard in some rhythm and blues lyrics. The first American rock stars, like Elvis Presley (above) or Bill Haley, studied the sounds of the blues and rhythm and blues. Young English rock artists like the Beatles and the Rolling Stones (below, Keith Richards) did the same. Their first concern was to revive the classics of the African-American tradition.

♦ **T-BONE WALKER** (1910–1975)
He was one of the most influential guitarists of the 1940s and 1950s. He was also a model for rock and roll guitarists.

♦ **THE JUKEBOX**
The jukebox was always present in bars in the ghettos, loudly playing rhythm and blues records.

♦ **RAY CHARLES**
(1932–)
A pianist, singer, and saxophonist, he emphasized the religious background of this music. A living legend of rhythm and blues, he is, along with James Brown, the forerunner of soul music.

♦ **JAMES BROWN**
(1928–)
In the heyday of rock and roll, the "Godfather of Soul" went back to the rhythmic roots of African-American music, whose sound he proudly imitated.

♦ **RHYTHM AND BLUES DANCING**
Acrobatic moves were as common among the musicians as they were among rhythm and blues dancers and audiences.

♦ **FROM THE GHETTO TO THE DOWNTOWN AREA**
People met in bars and clubs to socialize or to dance to the sound of a popular hit blaring out of the jukebox. Rhythm and blues replaced jazz, becoming the new sound of African-Americans and recording their moods and dreams.

A MODERN ART FORM

At the end of the 1940s, Charlie Parker and bebop were paving the way to the revision of jazz forms and conventions for other jazz artists. Tenor saxophonist Stan Getz's 1948 recording "Early Autumn" profoundly influenced many younger musicians. Jazz musicians acquired more and more awareness of their roles as artists and began to fight for the recognition of jazz as an art form equal to its European traditional counterpart. The enthusiasm for the research and experimentation of new musical idioms aroused in jazz musicians an interest in the other forms of expression. Therefore, jazz became a contemporary art form, a respected means of expression that reflected the changes in music.

♦ **GERRY MULLIGAN** (1927–1996) **AND CHET BAKER** (1929–1988)
They were pioneers in a successful quartet that had a quiet and airy style and was called West Coast Jazz.

♦ **THE MODERN JAZZ QUARTET**
Known since 1951, four musicians combined bebop with the counterpoint of the music of Bach and with contemporary music, always retaining swing and a passion for the blues.

♦ **THE BEAT GENERATION**
In the 1950s writers of the "beat generation" turned to jazz to protest against society.

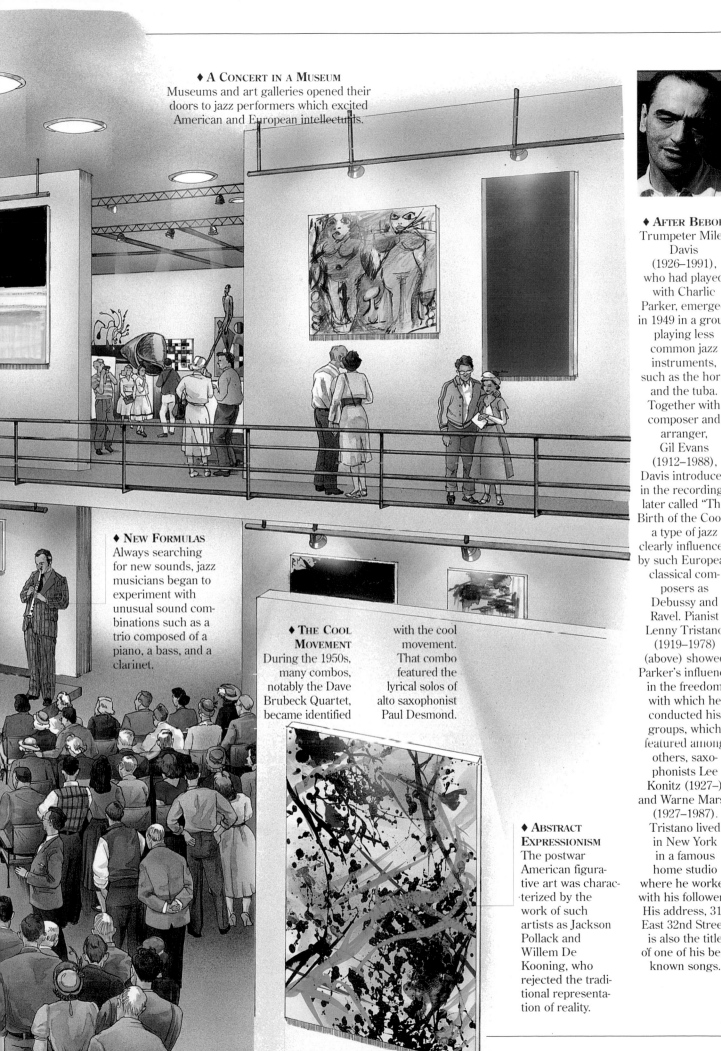

♦ **A Concert in a Museum**
Museums and art galleries opened their doors to jazz performers which excited American and European intellectuals.

♦ **After Bebop**
Trumpeter Miles Davis (1926–1991), who had played with Charlie Parker, emerged in 1949 in a group playing less common jazz instruments, such as the horn and the tuba. Together with composer and arranger, Gil Evans (1912–1988), Davis introduced in the recordings later called "The Birth of the Cool," a type of jazz clearly influenced by such European classical composers as Debussy and Ravel. Pianist Lenny Tristano (1919–1978) (above) showed Parker's influence in the freedom with which he conducted his groups, which featured among others, saxophonists Lee Konitz (1927–) and Warne Marsh (1927–1987). Tristano lived in New York in a famous home studio where he worked with his followers. His address, 312 East 32nd Street, is also the title of one of his best known songs.

♦ **New Formulas**
Always searching for new sounds, jazz musicians began to experiment with unusual sound combinations such as a trio composed of a piano, a bass, and a clarinet.

♦ **The Cool Movement**
During the 1950s, many combos, notably the Dave Brubeck Quartet, became identified with the cool movement. That combo featured the lyrical solos of alto saxophonist Paul Desmond.

♦ **Abstract Expressionism**
The postwar American figurative art was characterized by the work of such artists as Jackson Pollack and Willem De Kooning, who rejected the traditional representation of reality.

RECORDINGS

Since 1917, when the Original Dixieland Jazz Band recorded "Livery Stable Blues," records have narrated the history of jazz. They have become the best device to capture the originality of a performance, its unique flavor dictated by the artist's spirit of the moment. Recordings have stored the historical evolution of jazz, making its legacy available to future generations. Until the 1940s, records had been issued mostly by specialized record companies, independent from the industry giants. These new small companies were able to discover and promote the development of new creative trends and were also protagonists of the history of jazz.

♦ **FROM 78s TO CDs**
Various steps and different devices trace the history of recorded jazz, from the "race records" of the 1920s, conceived exclusively for the African-American market, to the elegant compact disc reissues that today present the work of the great legends. These crucial steps were the use of an electric recording system in 1926 and the magnetic recorder, which by means of a magnetic tape allowed lengthy recordings. This explains the switch from the ten-inch (25 cm) 78 rpm record that contained only a few minutes of music, to the twelve-inch (30 cm) 33 1/3 rpm record, the long-playing (LP) record that held almost twenty minutes of music on each side. In the early 1980s, digital technology introduced, at last, the compact disc, considered time-resistant and with a clear sound.

♦ **FROM THE STUDIO TO THE RECORD STORE**
A record is made by first recording the music in the recording studio. Mixing follows with the creation of the "master," and finally the printing of copies for distribution.

♦ **TECHNICAL SUPPORT**
The producer, who assists the musicians, and the sound engineer, who records the piece, are always present in the recording studio with the musicians.

Every cut, even the discarded versions, is numbered in order to identify it. These numbered cuts (takes) are then assembled in compilations, which document the creative progression of the artist.

Jazz Festivals

Festivals are intimately related to the history of jazz. The early ones were organized in Nice, France, in 1948, and in Paris in 1949. Their original purpose was to gather together, for a few days, the musicians who were not known by the European public because of the war. Both the public and the press regarded the festival as a big event. After their European success, festivals were widely organized in the 1950s in the United States. The Newport Jazz Festival, in Rhode Island, was one of the first. Jazz festivals are memorable musical events. Some festivals have become jazz institutions, and they all offer endless opportunities for the artists to express themselves.

♦ **A Triumph for Duke**
One of the most fulfilling events of the Newport Jazz Festival was Duke Ellington's band concert. In 1956 the performance of the song "Diminuendo and Crescendo in Blue" was met with great enthusiasm by the audience thanks to a tumultuous solo by the saxophonist Paul Gonzalves.

♦ **Tents, Sun, and a Lot of Music**
Festivals are outdoor events often held in the summer. A park can easily be turned into a jazz village, with bandstands, places to sell records, meeting places, and jazz-cafés.

♦ **The Protagonist**
Saxophonist, Paul Gonzalves (1920–1974), was one of the most talented and exuberant soloists in Duke Ellington's band.

♦ **Flashes On!**
Photographers were always prepared to capture unique musical moments.

♦ **Journalists and Headlines**
The press followed the festivals with great interest.

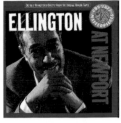

♦ ELLINGTON IN
NEWPORT
Ellington was
amazed by the
technical virtuosity
of his soloist and
stopped playing
the piano to
listen to him.

♦ THE NEWPORT
JAZZ FESTIVAL
Created by the
impresario and
musician, George
Wein, in 1954, the
Newport Jazz is
one of the most
famous jazz festi-
vals in the United
States. Many of
the concerts have
been recorded.
They represent
new successful
episodes in the
careers of Duke
Ellington, Miles
Davis, Thelonious
Monk, and Count
Basie. In 1958 the
movie director
Bert Stern shot
the movie *Jazz
on a Summer Day,*
in Newport. It
succeeded in
conveying to the
spectators the
breathtaking
atmosphere of the
show. In 1960 the
bassist, Charles
Mingus, and
drummer, Max
Roach, contested
the festival and
organized another
one, also in
Newport, with
a group of
musicians later
called the
"Newport Rebels."
In 1961, due to
violent conflicts,
the festival was
suspended for
the following
year. Since 1972
the festival has
also been held in
New York City.

♦ **SONNY ROLLINS**
(1930–)
His career started
during the bebop
era alongside
Charlie Parker
and Bud Powell,
from whom he
had inherited a
passion for the
research of an
authoritative
and distinct
instrumental
voice. The power-
ful sound of his
saxophone well
matched his
nickname of
"Saxophone
Colossus," which
was the title of
one of his records
in 1956. His
collaboration in
the same year
with trumpeter,
Clifford Brown
(1930–1956)
lasted only few
months due
to Brown's
premature death.
Rollins went on to
make some
remarkable
recordings such
as "Tenor
Madness" (1956),
with his colleague,
John Coltrane,
and "The
Freedom Suite"
(1958). Rollins is
still active today
and is one of the
most inspired
geniuses of jazz,
as he proved in
1985 during a
concert for solo
saxophone at
the Museum of
Modern Art in
New York, which
has been issued
as a record.

IN SEARCH OF AN IDENTITY

By the mid-1950s West Coast Jazz, a refined style
that diluted the African-American elements of this
music, had triumphed. In New York, African-
American musicians responded by returning to the
roots of jazz—from the blues and gospel came hard
bop, a tougher and cruder bop that was mastered
by Sonny Rollins, Thelonious Monk, Art Blakey,
and Miles Davis. This was a transitional period, during which the most typical instrumental jazz group,
the quintet, featuring trumpet, saxophone, piano,
double bass, and drums, predominated. The solos,
the nucleus of bebop performances, became longer
and longer, while arrangements became simpler.

♦ **ART BLAKEY**
(1919–1990)
One of the wildest jazz drummers,
his style was directly connected
to African polyrhythm. For three
generations, new jazz talents emerged
in his group, The Jazz Messengers.

♦ **BILL EVANS**
(1929–1980)
A white pianist admired by African-
American musicians, he collaborated
with Miles Davis on the masterpiece
"Kind of Blue." His 1960s trio inspired
the equality of the improvising roles,
a crucial step in modern jazz.

♦ **A POWERFUL RESONANCE**
Rollins decided to
play the saxophone
nights on the
Williamsburg
Bridge to maxi-
mize the power
of his saxophone
and to be con-
siderate to his
neighbors.
The experience
inspired his record
"The Bridge."

♦ **THELONIOUS MONK**
(1917–1982)
Although he was one of the promoters of the bebop revolution, the public ignored pianist and composer Thelonious Monk, for some time. He became known only during the second half of the 1950s, thanks to a series of important recordings in which he performed alongside saxophonists Sonny Rollins, Johnny Griffin (1928–), and Charlie Rouse (1924–1988). Monk is one of the most unpredictable central figures of jazz, an authentic mentor who underwrote several compositions, some of which have become jazz standards, thanks also to their interpretation by many jazz musicians. Among them are "Round Midnight" (1944), "Misterioso" (1948), and "Monk's Mood" (1957). A complex man, Monk was also noted for his eccentric ways, his long silences, and the unusual dances he improvised around the piano during concerts.

♦ **THE WILLIAMSBURG BRIDGE**
One of the four bridges that connect Manhattan Island to the contiguous States. It was completed in 1903, twenty years after another famous bridge, the Brooklyn Bridge. More than 240,000 people cross it every day.

SIGNS OF REVOLT

♦ THE BATTLE OF LITTLE ROCK
In the fall of 1957, to avoid riots and allow nine African-American students to attend classes at Little Rock High School, President Eisenhower sent in troops to enforce the court order.

♦ CHARLES MINGUS
(1922–1979)
One of the finest jazz bassists, he started his career in the 1940s with the giants of bop, Parker and Gillespie. He moved on to conduct his own bands, playing a full-bodied and intense music from which emerged the whole identity of jazz and its history. Blues and gospel music inspired Mingus. He experimented with Latin rhythms and reintroduced the collective improvisation, typical of early jazz, into modern jazz. From his masterpieces like "Pithecanthropus Erectus" (1956) to his later songs, Mingus poured himself into his music. He often had communication problems with his musicians because of his difficult, introverted, and sometimes irritable personality. Among his most faithful collaborators was drummer, Dannie Richmond (1935–1988), one of the few people with whom hc established a rewarding personal and artistic relationship.

Racism followed the African-Americans, and their music was often the most effective means they had to express their anger and sorrow for unbearable cruelty. Since the mid-1950s, acts of rebellion against discrimination and segregation have been numerous. In some cases, the protest was left to the creativity of such jazz musicians as Charles Mingus, who ironically dedicated his "Fables of Faubus" to Orval Faubus and his "fables." Governor of Arkansas in the second half of the 1950s, Faubus attempted to block the American government's policy of integration, which enforced combined classes of black and white students in schools.

♦ THE ANGRY CROWD
Under the orders of Faubus and Jimmy Karan, his assistant, agitators incited the crowd against the entrance of students at school. This caused riots, but ultimately the National Guard was able to regain control of the situation.

♦ BAYONETS AND BOOKS
For two days, soldiers escorted students to school until hostilities diminished.

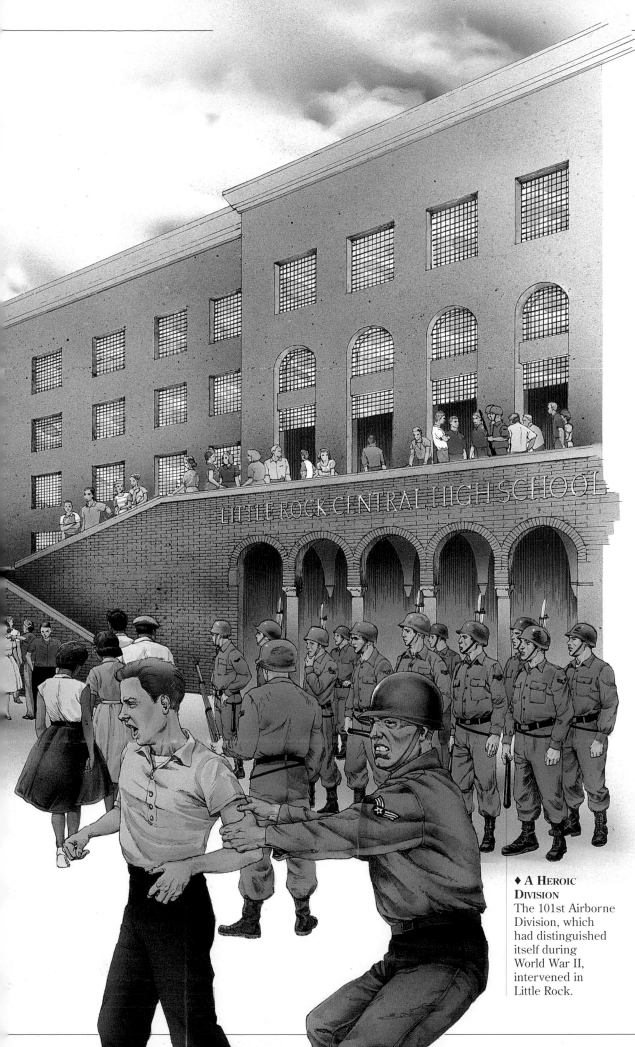

♦ **FREEDOM NOW!**
"We Insist! Freedom Now Suite" was the title chosen by drummer Max Roach for one of his works in 1960, where he explicitly used music to demand freedom and justice for his people. The record had some precedents in jazz like "Strange Fruit" (1939), by Billie Holiday, which dealt with a hanging of an African-American, and some ambitious works by Duke Ellington, who in 1943, had presented an articulate reflection in music with "Black, Brown and Beige." The richness of the African-American tradition is found in the music of saxophonist, "Rahsaan" Roland Kirk (1936–1977). Blind from the age of two, Kirk showed an extraordinary musical talent. In a concert he was capable of playing three saxophones, flutes, percussive instruments, and sirens, creating music of unique energy.

♦ **A HEROIC DIVISION**
The 101st Airborne Division, which had distinguished itself during World War II, intervened in Little Rock.

FREE JAZZ

♦ **ORNETTE COLEMAN**
(1930–)
A saxophonist, he was born in Texas, growing up in the heart of the blues tradition. He started playing the saxophone at fourteen. His career began in California. He moved to New York City with his friend, trumpeter Don Cherry (1936–1995), where he recorded "Free Jazz," the song that became the name of the jazz of the 1960s. This work featured the spontaneous improvisation of a double quartet of musicians and adopted Coleman's theories on musical freedom. Jazz was shaken up, just as in the past with Charlie Parker, who was often named by Coleman as one of his inspirations. His later experiments, ranging from electric ensembles to symphonic orchestras, reveal his creativity and originality.

In the 1960s jazz became a full-throated shout and with this music, the rage of the ghetto exploded. It was a result of the desperation of those living on the edge of society who see their rights abused every day. Protests and revolts shook the country and African-Americans followed their leaders: Martin Luther King, who appealed for nonviolence, and Malcolm X, with his messages that inflamed his followers. The music of these years was free jazz, unbound jazz, which advocated total freedom from the limits of harmony, and acquisition through the collective improvisation of a more precise African identity. Following Ornette Coleman's lucid theoretical lines or John Coltrane's mystical dimension, free jazz has radically modified the sound of jazz in the last thirty years.

♦ **ARCHIE SHEPP**
(1937–)
His saxophone was a powerful voice of the black revolt. His music reflected the influences of Africa, the messages of Malcolm X, the blues, and Duke Ellington.

♦ **ERIC DOLPHY**
(1928–1964)
Virtuoso of flute, alto sax, and bass clarinet, he collaborated with Coltrane and Mingus and was one of the most inspired artists of free jazz.

♦ **BLACK AND WHITE**
Groups of white protesters joined the revolutionary African-Americans.

♦ **CLUBS AND VIOLENCE**
The methods used by the police to disband protesters were often brutal.

♦ **BLACK POWER**
American cities were swept by African-American waves of protest. Washington, Chicago, and New York City were the scenes of violent riots erupting with the cry for black power.

♦ **SUN RA**
(1914–1993)
He said that he was born on another planet. He directed the most influential big band of the 1960s. His music, inspired by African rhythms and the symbols of ancient Egypt, fled from reality.

♦ **JOHN COLTRANE**
(1926–1967)
One of his first engagements was with Dizzy Gillespie's band. At this point in his life he was still perfecting his skills, but his talent would soon be discovered. Coltrane forever changed the method of playing both tenor and soprano saxophones. His innovation lay in the original idea that notes are linked together in continuous sequences. He played with his colleague, Sonny Rollins, and trumpeter, Miles Davis, before forming the famous quartet with McCoy Tyner (1938–) on piano, Jimmy Garrison (1934–1976) on bass, and Elvin Jones (1927–) on drums. This group recorded such masterpieces of jazz as "My Favorite Things" (1960), "Impressions" (1960), and "A Love Supreme" (1964), all with African and Indian influences, and inspired by a deep spirituality.

♦ **THE CAPITOL**
Demonstrations and protest marches ended up in front of the Capitol Building in Washington, D.C.

♦ **MALCOLM X**
(1925–1965)
One of the most authoritative and revolutionary leaders, he joined the Black Muslims (Nation of Islam), which was responsible for riots and demonstrations. He was assassinated while giving a speech in New York City, the victim of an obscure plot.

♦ **STREET BATTLES**
Revolts often degenerated into riots and city streets became battlefields.

ELECTRIC JAZZ

Around the mid-1960s, young people fell in love with rock. It became a hit with such new electric instruments as guitar, bass, piano, and organ. With its drive and openness, rock found its apotheosis in the enormous gatherings at Monterey, Woodstock, and the Isle of Wight, establishing itself as the sound track of an era, characterized by youth protest movements. It was the new idiom, able to overcome barriers and borders. Jazz, which was at first loved less by the general public, soon took hold of these new sounds. Miles Davis, sensitive to the spirit of the times, opened the way for the new music. And in the 1970s, many musicians blended jazz and rock music into fusion jazz.

♦ **LOVE, PEACE, AND MUSIC**
Rock concerts become magical and frantic scenes. Miles Davis was among the first to desert jazz clubs and concert halls for this more spectacular arena for his music.

♦ **JIMI HENDRIX**
(1942–1970)
Guitarist, singer, and composer, he remains a legend today. With his music, he glorified the bursting power of rock, reinterpreting the blues tradition.

♦ **THE CROWD**
Under the bandstand or on their feet, exuberant young crowds enjoy the concert.

♦ **WEATHER REPORT**
Saxophonist, Wayne Shorter (1933–), and keyboardist, Joe Zawinul (1932–), who played with Miles Davis, founded the famous group, Weather Report, in 1970.

♦ **ORGANS AND KEYBOARDS**
Instead of the traditional piano, there are now new keyboards, rich in various sound effects.

♦ **PLAY OF LIGHTS AND THOUSANDS OF WATTS**
Daylight illumination, multicolor lights, cables on the floor, and loud speakers make up the dazzling atmosphere of the concert.

♦ **THE INSTRUMENTS**
Typical rock music instruments, such as electric bass and guitar, found their place in jazz.

♦ **MILES DAVIS**
(1926–1991)
A renowned trumpeter, he achieved prominence playing with Charlie Parker during the bop years. He went through the various changes in modern jazz and was receptive to rock's electricity. In 1969 his record, "Bitches Brew," reflected the turning point of his musicianship. His obscure and visionary music adopted some of the sound suggestions of rock at that time. He appreciated Jimi Hendrix and his explosive remake of the blues, and James Brown and his messages of African-American assertiveness. Miles was influenced by them and elaborated on a type of music based on complex rhythmic textures and electric sounds not heard before in jazz. Soon, his colleagues, who created their own groups, followed his influence. Among them were the Mahavishnu Orchestra, directed by guitarist John McLaughlin (1942–), and the Headhunters, directed by pianist Herbie Hancock (1940–).

THE AVANT-GARDE

The free jazz revolution had shown the younger musicians the joys of experimenting. In the second half of the 1960s a new generation came forward that underscored the richness of the African-American tradition to the point of reinterpreting the origins of jazz in a free way. Its instrumental formulas were revolutionary: solo exhibitions, quartets of only saxophones, brass bands, and the use of unusual instruments. The musicians' constant research found inspiration in the sounds of early jazz as well as in contemporary academic music.

♦ STEVE LACY
(1943–)
The greatest modern specialist of the soprano saxophone, he is a disciple of Monk and was among the first to perform solo concerts, adopting a pure and quintessential style.

♦ THE AACM
One of the most stimulating centers of the new musical trend is located in Chicago. It is the Association for the Advancement of Creative Musicians (AACM), active since the mid-1960s. A new generation of jazz musicians, led by pianist Muhal Richard Abrams (1930–), belongs to this association. Its aim is to intensify the contacts among musicians and develop a critical perspective of the African-American musical tradition. Improvisation, which is now prompted by very complex techniques, is the revolutionary gesture by which artists manifest their independence from show business and, at the same time, the moment when their creativity is asserted. Some of its distinguished members are: the Art Ensemble of Chicago, founded in 1967 by among others trumpeter Lester Bowie (1941–), saxophonist Anthony Braxton (1945–) (above), and the trio Air, led by Henry Threadgill.

♦ ART ENSEMBLE OF CHICAGO
Today, with their original makeup and stage costumes, the five musicians of the Art Ensemble still emphasize the connection between jazz and other cultures and types of music around the world.

♦ LOFT JAZZ
Lofts, which are old and empty industrial spaces transformed into apartments or studios, have become the headquarters of the new music.

♦ THE SAXOPHONE FAMILY
The multi-instrumentalist, who plays and alternates different saxophones, is born.

♦ **INFORMALITY**
The autonomy of the new jazz is already evident in the informal atmosphere that surrounds every concert.

♦ **SOLO CONCERTS**
Musicians started to perform in solitude to free themselves from the music market.

♦ **HENRY THREADGILL**
(1944–)
One of the most remarkable saxophonists, flutists, and composers, in his various groups, he showed his debt to Jelly Roll Morton, Ellington, and Mingus.

JAZZ IN THE WORLD

Since the 1920s and the arrival of American musicians in Europe, jazz has been exported beyond the American shores. Its popularity has increased over the years through records, magazines, books, and movies, which, along with festivals and concerts, convinced musicians in other countries to follow the example of the Americans. Today, jazz is a universal idiom, popular everywhere in the world. One of the influences that has greatly contributed to its expansion is education. The oral tradition, typical of the beginning of jazz, has been replaced by a complex system of schools, where the works of the legends of jazz are analyzed and studied by students and professors.

♦ MOVIES AND JAZZ
The youngest of the forms of art and jazz have often come together. Films can offer a wide retrospective in images of the African-American musical evolution. The "soundies" of the 1930s, predecessors of videoclips, are short movies that present the cut live on the screen. Among the protagonists of soundies are: Louie Armstrong, Duke Ellington, Cab Calloway, and Billie Holiday. The documentary cinema is more detailed in its historical reporting of interviews, anecdotes, and performances. Jazz has also enhanced film narratives of the biographies of musicians with sound tracks. Among the well-known movies on jazz are: *The Cotton Club* (1984) by Francis Ford Coppola (above, a scene), *'Round Midnight* (1984) by Bertrand Tavernier, and *Bird* (1988) directed by Clint Eastwood, about the life and music of Charlie Parker.

♦ KEITH JARRETT
(1945–)
One of today's finest pianists still at work, he has helped to bring the world of jazz closer to classical music, from the music of Miles Davis to that of Johann Sebastian Bach.

♦ LEARNING RHYTHM AT SCHOOL
Those who take drum lessons get some exercise using pens and pencils as drumsticks.

♦ A MUSICIAN FOR A TEACHER
Musicians often teach their own techniques to students.

♦ NOTES AND SWING
Two beats for drums are written on the blackboard. Notations underline every rhythmic accent.

♦ ACCENTS AND RHYTHMS
A student practices on drums what the teacher is explaining.

♦ PAT METHENY
(1954–)
Virtuoso of the guitar, he is the promoter of a synthesis between jazz, rock, and other ethnic sounds.

♦ JAZZ IN SCHOOLS
In public and private schools, as well as in prestigious conservatories, it is possible to study jazz, practice an instrument or learn composition or arranging.

JAZZ IN THE YEAR 2000

At the threshold of the year 2000, jazz seems to be a tradition in progress, on a pace with the times, ready to enrich itself with various influences. More than ever, current proponents of jazz are careful to assimilate messages from other contemporary types of music. Today, jazz deals especially with the new rhythms of African-American music—rap and hip-hop—in which young African-Americans put aside traditional instruments and tell about life in the ghetto using electronic rhythms. Once again, jazz is used to narrate what surrounds it and it continues to portray a faithful account of true facts and the sound track of human experiences.

♦ **WYNTON MARSALIS**
(1961–)
He is the most respected trumpeter of contemporary jazz, at ease as a performer of baroque music as well as an improviser and jazz composer.

♦ **DON BYRON**
(1958–)
Clarinctist and composer, he is the author of a type of music of great versatility. He pays homage to the Yiddish repertoire of Mickey Katz, the sound of Ellington, and the Latin American musical rhythms.

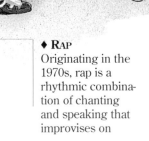

♦ **RAP**
Originating in the 1970s, rap is a rhythmic combination of chanting and speaking that improvises on words to famous songs, using only part of the original music as an accompaniment. It emphasizes rhythm over melody.

♦ **SINGING IN THE STREET**
Telling about their lives, young African-Americans have created a new world of sounds. A powerful rhythm allows them to sing freely, jamming in rhymes about everyday events.

♦ **JOSHUA REDMAN**
(1969–)
Virtuoso of the tenor saxophone, he is an intellectual who is able to retrace the most important moments of the history of his instrument in jazz.

♦ **STEVE COLEMAN**
(1956–)
Perhaps the most gifted protagonist of contemporary jazz, he is a composer, saxophonist, and sometimes singer and drummer. After a formative period with several groups, he started playing, in the early 1980s, with his favorite band, The Five Elements. Willing to enlarge the group for the sake of experimenting, the band often changed its name. Metrics, which reveals his relationship with rap, and Mystic Rhythm Society, a huge group that from time to time reunited musicians of the most diverse backgrounds, from Africa to Japan to Cuba. He is one of the most sought-after contemporary jazz musicians, always in great demand for collaborations. Among these collaborations is the remarkable one with Cassandra Wilson (1955–), one of today's most appreciated jazz singers.

♦ **NOW AND THEN**
Different generations of musicians study each other in a recurring and fruitful exchange of ideas and techniques.

♦ **HANDLING THE MUSIC**
Thanks to sophisticated technologies, a portable stereo, or "boombox," is capable of transforming the street into a concert hall.

CHRONOLOGY

1901 Louis Armstrong, the first great jazz soloist, was born in New Orleans. Starting at the end of the nineteenth century, New Orleans became the cradle of this new music, which blended the culture and musical sensitivity of the African slaves with that of the Europeans then present in America.

1917 The Original Dixieland Jazz Band, a musical group of white musicians, recorded for the first time in the history of jazz, "Livery Stable Blues." At the end of the year, the notorious Storyville district in New Orleans was closed, forcing musicians to move north.

1925 In Chicago, Louis Armstrong and his Hot Five began to record their hits. The fabulous blues singer, Bessie Smith, became the star of African-American music. The "Revue Nègre" opened in Paris featuring Josephine Baker, who was already a star at the Cotton Club.

1927 The orchestra of pianist and composer Duke Ellington was hired to play at the most famous nightclub in New York City, the Cotton Club, in Harlem. This district would host an artistic revival called the "Harlem Renaissance." Cab Calloway and Fats Waller also performed at the Cotton Club.

1935 Pianist William "Count" Basie began to play with his orchestra at the Reno Club, in Kansas City. His fame as a pianist, composer, and conductor soon spread. Soon 52nd Street in New York City became the place to go, with its many bars and nightclubs.

1938 On January 16, led by clarinetist and bandleader Benny Goodman, jazz entered one of the most prestigious temples of classical music: Carnegie Hall, in New York City. It was a crowded event, which celebrated the recognition of jazz as an art form.

1941 In New York, at the jazz club, Minton's Playhouse, the new proponents of jazz gathered in lively jam sessions. Among other participants were saxophonist Charlie Parker and trumpeter Dizzy Gillespie, two legends of the revolutionary bop.

1943 On January 1 at Carnegie Hall in New York City, Duke Ellington presented "Black, Brown and Beige," an ambitious work that honored the history of the African-American community, a musical appreciation of the values of his people.

1945 Bebop was now the new jazz. Charlie Parker recorded his first masterpieces. In the industrial cities of the North, rhythm and blues became the rage among African-American audiences. In Europe, jazz spread because of the V-Disc.

1948 The record industry introduced the twelve-inch (30 cm) 33 1/3 rpm record, the so-called long-playing (LP) record that contained almost twenty minutes of music per side and no longer "squeezed" solos. Recordings have stored the historical evolution of jazz.

1949 In Paris, jazz festivals continued to be popular with a program at "La Salle Pleyel." In New York City, the experiments of pianist, Lennie Tristano, and the works of trumpeter, Miles Davis and his nonet, defined the cool jazz trend.

1952 In California, a type of jazz with an airy and light rhythm and softened African-American elements, labeled West Coast Jazz, originated. It immediately became popular thanks to a quartet that included trumpeter Chet Baker and saxophonist Gerry Mulligan.

1956 Hard bop, represented by Art Blakey and the Jazz Messengers, reconnected jazz with the blues and the African-American tradition. Charles Mingus recorded "Pithecanthropus Erectus." African-Americans used jazz as a means to express their anger.

1960 Saxophonist Ornette Coleman recorded "Free Jazz," which became the manifesto of the new free and informal jazz. At the other extreme, famed saxophonist John Coltrane, composer of some fundamental jazz works, assembled his quartet.

1965 On May 8, in Chicago, the Association for the Advancement of Creative Musicians (AACM) was founded. Groups like Air and the Art Ensemble of Chicago, and soloists like saxophonist Anthony Braxton and pianist Muhal Richards Abrams were among its members.

1969 Trumpeter Miles Davis, who achieved prominence playing with Charlie Parker during the bop years, later opened jazz to electric instruments and rock rhythms with his recording of "Bitches Brew." Some of his closer colleagues, who created their own groups, followed his influence.

1976 The heirs of revolutionary free jazz generated loft jazz, a free and autonomous jazz played in the lofts of New York City, which were huge, empty, former industrial spaces transformed into studios and apartments; these became the "headquarters" of the new music.

1983 The CD (compact disc) was invented. It is a strong aluminum disc read by a laser beam, which replaced old vinyl discs. This invention was a new way to record the cuts that document the entire history of jazz.

DISCOGRAPHY

THE BLUES

The anthology, *Masters of the Delta Blues* (Yazoo) is a fundamental work.

ROBERT JOHNSON There are 29 blues songs on *The Complete Recordings* (Sony/Columbia).

BESSIE SMITH She sings in the five volumes of the *Complete Collection* (Sony/Columbia), accompanied by among others Louis Armstrong and Fletcher Henderson.

CLASSICAL JAZZ

SIDNEY BECHET His best recordings are part of *The Complete RCA Victor Recordings* (BMG).

FLETCHER HENDERSON His orchestra recordings are assembled in the collection *A Study in Frustration* (Sony/Columbia).

JELLY ROLL MORTON His best production is in *The Complete RCA Victor Recordings* (BMG), also alone on the piano, he recounts the origins of jazz during an interview in the recordings for the Library of Congress (Rounder).

LOUIS ARMSTRONG His first performances are recorded on CD under King Oliver (Milestone). His masterpieces as a solo artist, recorded since 1925, are in the four volumes of the series *Jazz Masterpieces* (Sony/Columbia).

DUKE ELLINGTON The 1920s–1930s recordings are assembled in *Early Ellington* (RCA/BMG) and *Okeh Recordings* (Sony Columbia). The mature recordings are in *The Blanton/Webster Years* (RCA/BMG) and *In the '40s: Black, Brown & Beige* (RCA/BMG).

THE SWING MUSIC AND SINGERS

COUNT BASIE The recordings of the 1930s are grouped in a set (Decca/GRP).

ELLA FITZGERALD Her mature works are in *The Cole Porter Songbook, The George Gershwin Songbook, The Ellington Songbook,* and *Ella and Louis* (Verve), the last one with Louis Armstrong.

BENNY GOODMAN The famous concert organized by the clarinetist at Carnegie Hall in 1938 is on CD (Sony Columbia).

COLEMAN HAWKINS His main recordings, including the famous "Body and Soul," are on *Body and Soul* (BMG).

BILLIE HOLIDAY Her production between the 1930s and 1940s is assembled in an eight-volume series, *Jazz Masterpieces* (Sony/Columbia). *The Complete Commodore Recordings* (Commodore/GRP) and the whole collection of the Verve recordings, portraying the 1950s (Verve/Polygram), are noteworthy.

GLENN MILLER The best musical collection of the trombonist and conductor is on *The Genius of Glenn Miller* (BMG).

JAZZ AT THE PHILHARMONIC The best concerts are on CD (Pablo).

FRANK SINATRA The celebrated *Songs for Swingin' Lovers* and *A Swingin' Affair* are a must. He made a great number of successful albums and CDs.

ART TATUM *Art Tatum Meets Ben Webster* (Pablo) and *The Complete Pablo Solo Masterpieces* (Pablo).

BEBOP

DIZZY GILLESPIE The recordings of the 1940s are in *The Savoy Sessions* (Savoy). *Birks Works* (Verve/Polygram) of the 1950s, with his big orchestra, is noteworthy. A series of duets with the saxophonists Sonny Rollins and Sonny Stitt are on *For Music Only* (Verve/Polygram).

THELONIOUS MONK The first works of the pianist are recorded in *Genius of Modern Music* (Blue Note).

CHARLIE PARKER His production of the 1940s is assembled in *The Savoy Sessions* (Savoy) and in *The Dial Masters* (Stash). A set of ten CDs (Verve/Polygram) contains the recordings of the 1950s.

BUD POWELL Five volumes (Blue Note) document his most important works.

COOL JAZZ AND WEST COAST JAZZ

MILES DAVIS *The Birth of the Cool* (Capitol EMI) documents the trumpeter's nonet.

CHET BAKER His best songs of the 1950s are on *The Pacific Jazz Years* (Pacific Jazz/EMI). The recordings of the famed quartet with Chet Baker and Gerry Mulligan are on *Mulligan & Baker* (Prestige).

MODERN JAZZ QUARTET *Django* (Prestige) and *The Last Concert* (Atlantic) are recommended collections.

LENNIE TRISTANO Key songs of the pianist are in the compilation, *Intuition* (Capitol).

TOWARD FREE JAZZ

ART BLAKEY With his group, The Jazz Messengers, he recorded such hit collections as *A Night in Tunisia* (Blue Note).

MILES DAVIS *Miles Ahead, Sketches of Spain,* and *Porgy & Bess* (Sony/Columbia), recorded with Gil Evans's orchestra, is an enjoyable selection. The records for small groups such as *Milestone* and *Kind of Blue* (Sony/Columbia) are also milestones.

BILL EVANS His trio is at its best in *Waltz for Debbie* (Riverside).

CHARLES MINGUS *Pithecanthropus Erectus, Oh Yeah, Blues and Roots,* and *The Clown* (Atlantic) are his most remarkable compositions.

THELONIOUS MONK *Brilliant Corners, Thelonious Himself,* and *Live at the Five Spot* (Riverside) are touchstones of the jazz of the 1950s.

MAX ROACH His activity is documented by the following records: *Alone Together* (Mercury/Verve), with trumpeter Clifford Brown, and by the important *We Insist! Freedom Now Suite* (Candid).

SONNY ROLLINS *Saxophone Colossus* (Prestige), *The Freedom Suite* (Riverside), and *The Bridge* (RCA/BMG) are key works.

FREE JAZZ

ORNETTE COLEMAN All the recordings of his quartet and the famous *Free Jazz* are compiled in the set *Beauty Is a Rare Thing—The Complete Atlantic Recordings* (Atlantic).

JOHN COLTRANE His first masterpieces are *My Favorite Things* and *Olé Coltrane* (Atlantic), followed by the notable *A Love Supreme, Africa/Brass, Impressions, Plays Ballads, Kulu Se Mama,* and *Selflessness* (Impulse).

SUN RA He is accompanied by his orchestra in *Jazz in Silhouette* (Evidence) and *The Heliocentric World of Sun Ra*, volumes 1 & 2 (ESP).

ARCHIE SHEPP The saxophonist is at his best in *Four for Trane, Fire Music,* and *The Way Ahead* (Impulse).

ELECTRIC JAZZ

MILES DAVIS *Bitches Brew* (Sony/Columbia) is historic. The following works are also important: *Live Evil* and *Live at Fillmore* (Sony/Columbia). Notable works by groups directed by former collaborators of Davis are: the *Weather Report* with Weather Report and *I Sing the Body Electric* (Sony/Columbia), and the Mahavishnu Orchestra with *The Inner Mounting Flame* and *Birds of Fire* (Sony/Columbia).

FROM AVANT-GARDE TO TODAY

MUHAL RICHARD ABRAMS He has issued the recent *Think All Focus One* and *Song for All* (Soul Note).

ART ENSEMBLE OF CHICAGO The group is at its best in *Fanfare for the Warriors* (Atlantic) and *Great Black Music* (DIW).

DON BYRON *Tuskeegee Experiments* and *Bug Music* (Nonesuch) are noteworthy.

ANTHONY BRAXTON He is documented by *Eight (+3) Tristano Compositions* (Hat Art) and *The London Concert* (Leo).

STEVE COLEMAN His best works, close to rap and the Cuban traditions, are *The Way of the Cypher* and *The Sign and the Seal* (BMG).

KEITH JARRETT Key works are his successful series trio, *Standards* (ECM), as well as solo piano improvisations like the recent *La Scala* (ECM) recorded at the well-known theater in Milan.

STEVE LACY Not to be missed is *Live at the Dreher* (At Art), featuring his duets with pianist Mal Waldron.

WYNTON MARSALIS *City Movements* and the ambitious creation, *Blood on the Fields* (Sony/Columbia), are distinguished works.

PAT METHENY He has recorded *Song X* (Geffen) with Ornette Coleman, and *The Road to You* (Geffen) with his band.

JOSHUA REDMAN Listen to his *Moodswing* (Warner Brothers).

HENRY THREADGILL His last works are *Carry the Day* and *Where's Your Cup?* (Sony/Columbia).

INDEX